TOOLS FOR CAREGIVERS

- **F&P LEVEL:** B
- **WORD COUNT:** 21
- **CURRICULUM CONNECTIONS:** animals, habitats, nature

Skills to Teach

- **HIGH-FREQUENCY WORDS:** a, has, in, is, it
- **CONTENT WORDS:** climbs, eats, forest, fur, panda, paws, plays, sleeps
- **PUNCTUATION:** periods
- **WORD STUDY:** long /a/, spelled ay (*plays*); long /e/, spelled ea (*eats*); long /e/, spelled ee (*sleeps*)
- **TEXT TYPE:** information report

Before Reading Activities

- Read the title and give a simple statement of the main idea.
- Have students "walk" through the book and talk about what they see in the pictures.
- Introduce new vocabulary by having students predict the first letter and locate the word in the text.
- Discuss any unfamiliar concepts that are in the text.

After Reading Activities

Explain to readers that pandas are bears. What other kinds of bears can readers name? How are panda bears similar to other bears, such as polar bears, black bears, or grizzly bears? How are they different?

Tadpole Books are published by Jump!, 5357 Penn Avenue South, Minneapolis, MN 55419, www.jumplibrary.com

Copyright ©2024 Jump. International copyright reserved in all countries. No part of this book may be reproduced in any form without written permission from the publisher.

Editor: Jenna Gleisner **Designer:** Emma Almgren-Bersie

Photo Credits: GlobalP/iStock, cover; Eric Isselee/Shutterstock, 1, 2mr, 4–5; Hung Chung Chih/Shutterstock, 2tl, 8–9; Ninel Roshchina/Alamy, 2tr, 10–11; clkraus/Shutterstock, 2ml, 2bl, 3, 6–7; Donyanedomam/Dreamstime, 2br, 12–13; Lee Yiu Tung/Shutterstock, 14–15; sanjagrujic/Shutterstock, 16tl; Menno Schaefer/Shutterstock, 16tr; FloridaStock/Shutterstock, 16bl; Rita_Kochmarjova/Shutterstock, 16br.

Library of Congress Cataloging-in-Publication Data
Names: Deniston, Natalie, author.
Title: Pandas / by Natalie Deniston.
Description: Minneapolis, MN: Jump!, Inc., (2024)
Series: My first animal books | Includes index.
Audience: Ages 3–6
Identifiers: LCCN 2022054068 (print)
LCCN 2022054069 (ebook)
ISBN 9798885246767 (hardcover)
ISBN 9798885246774 (paperback)
ISBN 9798885246781 (ebook)
Subjects: LCSH: Pandas—Juvenile literature.
Classification: LCC QL737.C27 D465 2024 (print)
LCC QL737.C27 (ebook)
DDC 599.789—dc23/eng/20221110
LC record available at https://lccn.loc.gov/2022054068
LC ebook record available at https://lccn.loc.gov/2022054069

MY FIRST ANIMAL BOOKS

PANDAS

by Natalie Deniston

TABLE OF CONTENTS

Words to Know 2

Pandas 3

Let's Review! 16

Index 16

WORDS TO KNOW

climbs

eats

forest

fur

paws

plays

PANDAS

A panda is in a forest.

fur

4

It has fur.

It has paws.

It climbs.

It eats.

It plays.

It sleeps.

LET'S REVIEW!

Pandas are bears. Can you point to the other bears below?

INDEX

climbs 9
eats 11
forest 3
fur 5

paws 7
plays 13
sleeps 15